Prayerful Pauses
Finding God's Presence in Daily Life

AMY WELBORN

TWENTY-THIRD PUBLICATIONS
A Division of Bayard
One Montauk Avenue, Suite 200
New London, CT 06320
(860) 437-3012 or (800) 321-0411
www.23rdpublications.com

Cover image © Photos.com, a division of Getty Images.

ISBN 978-1-58595-782-8
Library of Congress Control Number: 2010942703
Printed in the U.S.A.

CONTENTS

Easter to Pentecost

Festivals

Ordinary Time

Introduction

If there's one word that comes to me when I consider the ways in which God speaks to me, it's this one: *Surprise.*

It's never when you expect it and it's hardly ever what you expect to hear. Consider these moments from Scripture:

Sitting outside your tent with your elderly wife inside, three strangers approach.

Tending your father-in-law's sheep on a mountain, an ordinary bush in the distance.

Fishing, repairing nets, counting the day's catch.

Walking to the well to fetch water, as you've done every day, as you expect you will do for the rest of your life.

At dinner in your house, with guests both invited and not.

Sitting in your house in your small village, far away from anyone important, contemplating whatever it is young women contemplate in such a time and place.

Surprise.

The spiritual life, it seems to me, is nothing more than learning to listen and be open to that surprising presence of God. It's not easy, though. It takes a lifetime—and more.

Because people are different, we have various ways of drawing closer to God, recognizing God's voice, and learning to listen.

I've found that for me, the act of writing has helped me a great deal.

For over twenty years, I've done the sort of spiritual writing you will read in these pages, looking at the intersection of faith and life. In the midst of the deadlines, I have learned to listen.

On a prosaic level, I always need to keep my eyes open for material, but that necessity deepens my faith life in the process. In fact, when I don't have a project involving that kind of writing in the hopper, I find that my spiritual life suffers. I'm just not as alive and aware, intent on making those connections between what's just happened and God's will.

I think it's the same way for any of us engaged in our daily tasks—if we want to find meaning and God's presence in those tasks, we must seek it and be open to it.

My process in doing this kind of writing reflects this, too. Most of the time it begins, not with a Scripture passage or a saint's life, but brainstorming over my own life. I look through my journal. I check out the piece of paper I have tacked to the bulletin board on which I've scribbled significant experiences— amusing, ironic, sad, confusing, or comforting—here, there, and everywhere. And then I turn to God's word, and let the connections happen.

Is that the only way? No, of course not. But for me, it's how I try to avoid being preachy or didactic. All I really want to do is share, to point, to move a reader to do the same. Above all, I just hope to sit with you as we lay out our lives in joy and tears before the God who surprises—and listen.

Amy Welborn
Winter 2010

Advent and Christmas

Prayerful pauses

Be patient, therefore, brothers, until the coming of the Lord. See how the farmer waits for the precious fruit of the earth, being patient with it until it receives the early and the late rains.

JAMES 5:7

I gave a talk in a parish on prayer a few months ago and spoke a bit about what I call "monastic time." That is, prayer in a monastery is much different than it is, say, in a normal parish, and not just because it happens around the clock. Prayer in a monastery is…relaxed. It is deliberate. There is absolutely no rush. There are pauses between the lines of prayers and between responses.

At the end of my talk, the pastor suggested that the group pray the Lord's Prayer on "monastic time": slowly, pausing between the stanzas.

It was hard. The pull to just jump into the next line without even a breath was fierce and difficult to resist. But gradually, we fell into the rhythm and learned patience. The pull to see what comes next is strong, in prayer and life. But the Lord tells us: patience. Let go. In the pauses, in the silence, in the waiting, he does his work.

Lord, teach me patience
as I wait for you.

Speaking the truth

When the people in the synagogue heard this, they were all
filled with fury. They rose up, drove him out of the town...
LUKE 4:28-29

At a playground, a group of girls—part of the large Burmese
immigrant group that gathered there every Sunday—rushed up
to a man pushing his baby in a swing. "Can you help us?" they
asked. "Those boys won't stop throwing mulch at us."

So the man left his post and spoke strongly to the two boys,
who simply made faces and vaguely rude gestures, then some
things in a foreign language, and ran away. One of the girls
sighed. "He was cursing at you in Burmese." And then she, too,
along with her own posse, drifted away.

Jesus had the opposite problem. Those he knew quite well—
his own people—rejected him in words and actions he could
understand quite well. The truth is hard to hear. It's even harder
to speak, knowing how it's usually received, isn't it?

Lord Jesus, strengthen me
to speak of you in truth and love.

"Do not fear, I am with you"

*Then…the angel of the Lord appeared to him, standing at
the right of the altar of incense. Zechariah was troubled
by what he saw, and fear came upon him.*

LUKE 1:10-12

There's much to ponder in the story of John the Baptist's conception and birth. There is a powerful continuity with the past, as we're reminded of other miraculous births—Samson, for example. We're moved to consider Zechariah's faith—and our own—in the presence of God and his ways. But the whole scene becomes even more powerful when we consider what follows it.

We are far from the Holy City, in the home of a girl no one has ever heard of, a girl who would never be able to glimpse the door of the Holy of Holies, much less enter it. Within her, God moves. God does as he will, and here he wills to break through the walls, come to his people, dwell in his own creation, as a zygote embedded in the womb of this anonymous girl. And to her—and us—the angel says, "Do not be afraid."

Jesus, in your presence with me,
I am not afraid.

Acceptance with love

The book of the genealogy of Jesus Christ,
the son of David, the son of Abraham.

MATTHEW 1:1

The genealogies in Luke and Matthew fascinate me. On the surface, they're just a list of names. But I always think, with writing materials in the first century in short supply, the evangelists must have had excellent reasons for taking up space with Jesus' family tree. Maybe it was to emphasize Jesus' humanity and his role in Israel's history.

On a more prosaic level, it seems I can learn something else here: Jesus embraced humanity. Mysteriously, the word became flesh and accepted all that came with it, out of love. What about my family tree and all of its baggage? Sometimes I find myself wanting to run from it, excising all of that messiness that courses through my veins. I can't do that, though. Sure, I'm not fated to anything. I can be transformed, I can take a different turn in the road. But total rejection? Not possible. It's all a part of who I am. With God's help I can discern, move forward, and even accept. Out of love—I can accept.

Jesus, teach me through
my own family tree.

Ask questions...then listen

So they asked him, "What are you then?
Are you Elijah....Are you the Prophet?"

JOHN 1:21

Making conversation is an art, and I've known my share of folks who just can't do it. I've spent some time pondering this—partly to teach my kids simple social skills—and I've decided that the core of it is all about asking questions. The worst conversationalists, it seems, are unable to move outside of themselves and actually ask a question of another person in the room.

But questions are more than useful conversation starters. Those gathered at the River Jordan peppered John the Baptist with questions and so learned about the One to come, their savior. Think of how many of Jesus' parables were told in response to a question.

The first few paragraphs of one of the greatest prayers of all, St. Augustine's *Confessions*, is nothing but questions for God. What would our prayer be like if we asked more questions? If we set aside our interior monologues, let the questions we have emerge, and then...listened?

Father, I come to you with the
questions burning in my heart.

Step back and pray

The Lord is good to all,
compassionate to every creature.

PSALM 145:9

One of my older sons called me with a problem. Actually, he called me several times with the same problem. This went on for a while. At one point, he revealed a detail about the situation, something he'd not told me in hours of hashing things out.

"Well, of course," I said, "That explains everything."

And it did. It was one of those things that I thought anyone could see. But no, apparently not. He couldn't see the sad truth. There was a door in all of this to which he—and probably no other human being—held a key. But he had convinced himself that good intentions and compassion could fix things.

Sometimes it's difficult to arrive at that point when we need to understand that we've done as much as we can do for another person. It's hard and painful, but at times necessary, to step back and pray that God's compassion, which is faithful and real, will touch another's heart, even if we have to step aside in the process.

Lord, touch those in need
in my life with your compassion.

"Oh, how God loves us!"

Blessed be the Lord, the God of Israel,
for he has visited and brought
redemption to his people.

LUKE 1:68

The weight of it is beyond human words, the truth of this Word made flesh. In the abstract it is a puzzle and a difficulty to some, but when we attach the truth to the sight of a real baby, perhaps the one peering at us over his father's shoulder in church, or the one on our very own lap, it is enough to send you reeling. Oh, how God loves us.

And he comes to us, not to condemn or judge, but to redeem, to save. That is sometimes hard for us to grasp, so accustomed are we to the modern opinion that religion exists to restrict and confine.

But redemption it is. Salvation is what we find when we embrace the baby and let ourselves be embraced in turn. Freedom from whatever binds us to darkness. Release from the sins that burden us, a shattering of the chains that keep us at a careful, regretful distance from real love and peace.

From what prison do we seek freedom tonight?

Lord God, thank you for the gift of the Word made flesh. Help me embrace the freedom you bring in the Child Jesus.

Lack of faith leaves me speechless

Immediately his mouth was opened,
his tongue freed, and he spoke blessing God.

LUKE 1:64

Poor Zechariah, speechless during the most miraculous months of his long life. Within moments of hearing the grand news of the birth of a child to him and his aging wife Elizabeth, he was struck mute, unable to share his joy in words.

The loss and the restoration of Zechariah's speech were related to his acceptance of God's will. The angel Gabriel took his speech because Zechariah expressed doubt, and it was restored because Zechariah gave the child the name God had chosen: John.

Much to my own regret and shame, I've too often fallen speechless when the faith I claim to espouse is denigrated or my values are mocked. It is a lack of faith and trust that puts me there. I have a hard time trusting that God means what he says—that his truth and love will sustain me in a way that other people's opinion of me won't.

And when I finally do decide to trust, the funniest thing happens: I can speak again.

Lord, help me to trust in you and share
your love with honesty and courage.

Lament for fame that never came

She hears no voice,
accepts no correction.
ZEPHANIAH 3:2

For weeks a while back, I had been trying to get on television, with no luck. There was a lot of Catholic news going on—old pope, new pope, pop culture matters—and I'd been contacted. I'd been thinking and hoping this would be really good for my career.

I'd come close about six times, but no luck. Cable news called several times, but there were conflicts: there wasn't the right connection at our television station or I was going to be out of town. I even made it as far as New York City, filming a segment for a show—that got cut a day before the scheduled airing.

Meanwhile, I watched others get their moment. It irritated me. In fact, you might say I'd been taken back to fourth grade again, jealous of the other little girl who got to go to Disneyland.

Which, I can't help suspecting, might have had something to do with why these things kept falling through. Maybe the limelight was not the kind of light I needed.

Heavenly Father, help me turn my
frustrations into moments of growth.

13

Rational acts of kindness

Behold, I am the handmaid of the Lord.
LUKE 1:38

I tend too often to think of my faith in only the boldest strokes and biggest gestures. I live in such a culture of achievement and success, I absorb the idea that this is what makes a life good.

I was recently waiting to make a purchase in a department store, trying to handle my squirmy five-month-old and ever-restless four-year-old. The elderly woman ahead of us was taking a while, and I was working hard at hiding my impatience with everyone.

The white-haired woman noticed my children and started talking to the older one. By that time, he was rummaging around in my purse and had removed my cell phone. She reached into her purse, took out her own, and proceeded to "call" my son, keeping him occupied for the remaining time.

Such a little thing, but such a helpful thing, such an act of loving service to someone she didn't even know.

Jesus, may I find moments to serve you
and others in small ways today.

These (busy) "days to come"

In days to come…

ISAIAH 2:2

This is just what we're thinking about as Advent begins, isn't it? All of the "days to come" from now until Christmas.

For many of us, the struggle will be the same we've gone through in years past: trying to hold the line against the pressures to entertain, to be entertained, to purchase gifts, to cook, to decorate. They are intense. We know we should be attending to our spiritual lives above all, preparing the way for the Lord in our own hearts…but when?

In days to come.

Notice what Isaiah says will happen "in days to come." Not: You will do things that will please others. Not: You will achieve and accomplish. Not: You will earn God's favor. No, in "days to come" God will give a great gift.

Perhaps that clears a path through the busyness. In days to come, we might let go, listen, and let God work wonders.

Lord, in days to come,
fill my heart with joy.

I am not alone

O people of Zion, who dwell in Jerusalem,
no more will you weep.
ISAIAH 30:19

Our four-year-old son is in an all-day preschool, and has had no trouble through most of the year. As I write this, the year is two months away from its end, and the teacher is concerned because Joseph is breaking out into tears at the drop of a hat.

"He's four," my husband says. "When I was in first grade, I was wetting my pants. He's way ahead of me."

Well, it's still not the best situation. So I have been wracking my brain trying to figure out the reason. I got a clue when the other day, the teacher told me after school that she was proud of him. He had been tempted to cry when someone was bothering him, but instead spoke up and asked the other child to stop—something, I'm guessing, he was afraid to do before, and his frustration built to the point of tears.

He wept because he thought there was nothing he could do, and he was alone in his sadness and frustration. That's why a lot of us weep. God has an answer for that: his loving presence. We're not alone at all.

God, I pour out my sadness before you.
I trust in your love to bring me joy.

16

Brave witnesses from the past

Be vigilant at all times and pray that you have the strength to escape the tribulations that are imminent and to stand before the Son of Man.

LUKE 21:36

In Rome, martyrs are everywhere: statues and paintings depicting their sacrifices, names etched into churches built on their graves or places of execution. Lawrence, Agnes, Cecilia, and, of course, Peter and Paul.

I eventually came to terms with what initially struck me as a contradiction between the poverty of these martyrs and their elaborate memorials, for these churches ended up speaking to me more forcefully of strength than excess. The story of Agnes, for example, tells of a young teenage girl who bravely faced death rather than deny Christ. A teenager!

Through her witness, the Good News was preached. The strong, complicated, enduring buildings symbolize the Church that flourishes because these martyrs listened to Jesus and were vigilant and strengthened through prayer.

Am I?

God, during this Advent season, may I be strengthened to witness to the Good News of the Word made flesh.

Christmas surprises

*Do not be afraid, Zechariah, because your prayer
has been heard. Your wife Elizabeth will bear
you a son, and you shall name him John.*

LUKE 1:13

John is one of many surprising babies in Scripture. Sarah bore Isaac in her old age. The first reading for today's Mass tells us the story of Samson's birth, and during Advent we also hear of Samuel, whose mother Hannah's hymn of praise to God for her child echoes centuries later in Mary's Magnificat, the song of the mother of the most surprising child of all: Jesus, Son of God, born of a poor virgin in a quiet corner of the mighty Roman Empire, Savior of the world.

If you think about it, every child is a surprise, even those born in the most normal, unexceptional circumstances. We talk about planning such things, but of course, you can't plan a person and the surprises he or she brings.

We come to Christmas sometimes thinking we know the story because we have heard it so many times before. After twenty, thirty, forty, or sixty Christmases, what can be new? You never know. Jesus is coming. Be ready to be surprised.

Lord Jesus, bring something new
and joyful into my life.

I'm created and saved out of love

My lover speaks; he says to me,
"Arise, my beloved, my beautiful one,
and come!"

SONG OF SONGS 2:10

Beware of what you say to a mother when she is irritated. Even declarations of love can get you scolded. How many times one of my young children says to me, "I love you, Mommy," and my instinctive, smart-aleck response is, "Well, if you love me, you'll do what I say." Or they ask me what I would like for a gift, and I say, half-joking, "All I want is a good boy."

Half-joking.

The Scriptures are a love story. From Genesis to Revelation, they are the story of this lover—God—creating us out of love and continually reaching out to us in love, rescuing us from our self-inflicted misery and pain. In love, coming to us in a form that we finally cannot resist—who, after all, can not love a baby?

It is love, not anything else. And as I turn to the Lord in gratitude for this gift, and I myself utter a word of love, my own words, oddly, echo back to me: "If you love me…"

God, grateful for your love,
I listen to your word and follow.

Lent

Is my faithfulness fading?

*Faithfulness has disappeared; the word itself
is banished from their speech.*

JEREMIAH 7:28

I have two young adult sons who have been absorbed, over the past few years, making all kinds of the decisions young people have to make: what to major in, what career to follow, what to do in relationships, how to spend their money, and more. They're good young men, but over the years, something dawned on me: as they (endlessly) discussed their problems with me, God hardly ever entered the picture.

As they worked through their decisions, their criteria didn't seem to be much different from any other kid raised without reference to God. Of course, that depressed me, since I had something to do with how they thought about these things. So in our conversations I began to try to remedy this, to reintroduce questions of vocation, God's will and purpose into their speech, something that had disappeared.

And in the process, of course, I had to consider my own goals and hopes for life. It's one thing to worry about my sons' framework, but what about my own?

Lord, you are at the center of my life.
Guide me in all I do.

Allowing God's love to fill us

What can I do with you, Ephraim?...Your piety is like
a morning cloud, like the dew that early passes away.

HOSEA 6:4

What can God do with me, indeed? No, my name isn't Ephraim, but how many times have I grabbed onto a spiritual practice, declared that this is it and that when I do this right, I'll be right with God?

Lent is good for that. Happens all the time. Why? Well, sometimes a spiritual practice truly isn't right for us. Even St. Thérèse had trouble saying the rosary. There is also the issue of discipline. How quickly the thoughts race in, "Oh, does God really care about this? He knows my heart, and that's enough!" But sometimes there's something else called pride. Our piety comes and goes because we treat it as something like working out or dieting: an accomplishment achieved through our own efforts.

Holiness is not about us. It's about letting God's love and life fill us. That takes discipline and attentiveness, true, but neither is it something we do on our own. Let God be God in my life. That's holiness, and that never passes away.

Loving God, live in me
and love through me.

Nourishment beyond measure

I am the bread of life; whoever comes to me will never hunger, and whoever believes in me will never thirst.

JOHN 6:35

In the pew ahead of us at Mass were a mother and her younger teenaged son. Never has a boy looked so sorry to be in church. He slouched, he stood sideways with a foot on the pew instead of facing forward, he glowered—at us, it seemed—from time to time.

At the end, after communion, after we had been told to go in peace, as his mother opened her hymn book, the boy moved in her direction. She pointed to the words. He never opened his mouth, but his head remained bent, his gaze focused on the page. Their shoulders touched.

I can't presume to know anything certain about what I saw. But I can't deny that what I thought—or perhaps hoped—I saw was like the renewed energy produced by good, healthy food. Nourished by the "Bread of life," the door was opened to love.

Jesus, Bread of life,
feed me.

The bread that satisfies all hungers

...the Lord Jesus, on the night he was handed over,
took bread, and, after he had given thanks, broke it and said,
"This is my body that is for you. Do this in remembrance of me."
1 CORINTHIANS 11:23-24

Have you ever drifted through your kitchen, grazing? Have you ever wandered the grocery store, vaguely hungry, unable to commit? There's an emptiness inside—you know that—but what will satisfy it is another question completely.

Sometimes we drift in just that way through days, weeks, and months of life. We try this and that, we put our minds and hearts to various activities that we think will satisfy us. But we're still hungry. What can we find now that will fill us, at least for a while?

We gather at the Lord's table, each bearing our own hungers, some we can articulate, others we cannot. We are grieving, we are lost, we are confused, we are lonely. But somehow, with all of these various needs, we have all ended up at the same place, looking to the same Bread to feed us.

And the miracle is—God will.

Lord, thank you for the
gift of yourself in the Eucharist.

Everybody has a story

*...for he makes his sun rise on the bad and the good,
and causes rain to fall on the just and the unjust.*

MATTHEW 5:45

Looking down on the earth from the window of an airplane, I am struck by the beauty and variety of the land. I'm amazed and grateful that somehow I am mysteriously (at least to me) being held aloft at such a height.

As I pass over cities and towns, I can't help but be awed and humbled by the fact that each one of the thousands of homes in my sight contains a story—or even a few—as many intricate, joyful, and painful stories as there are people inside.

And God created each one of those people who are living out the stories of their lives, created them out of love. God is watching over each one, intimately involved in each life, whispering through each conscience, waiting patiently for each heart to open to his love.

I'm reminded that I'm not the center of the universe. God's love embraces all of us. And, within the limitations of my humanity, so should mine.

Lord, today I pray for those
I don't like or understand.

Funny money

Ask and it will be given to you...
MATTHEW 7:7

For years, my oldest son and I had a running joke. He'd say to me, out of the blue, apropos of nothing, "Can I have a dollar?" I'd always say no.

This went on for a long time. He'd ask me at the grocery store, when I picked him up at school. The joke, I suppose, was ultimately about my stinginess. Of course, I wouldn't just give him a dollar for no reason. That wouldn't be like me. So asking for what you knew you wouldn't get would be funny, I guess.

One night, we came out of the movies. As we got to the car, he asked.

"Can I have a dollar?"

I whipped out a bill from my pocket and handed it to him. He stood, stunned, and then laughed. Now this was really funny. After all these years, he finally got his dollar.

We, too, might be surprised by God's unexpected answers to our prayers.

Loving God, today I present my needs
to you and trust in your answer.

God knows our needs

Your Father knows what you need before you ask him.
MATTHEW 6:8

If you've ever worked in a specific field for any length of time, you know that there are only so many questions that you're going to be asked.

A workshop leader at a pro-life gathering once told aspiring public speakers that there were really only about fifteen questions—or variations thereof—that they'd ever hear. Schoolteachers improve with age and experience because they can anticipate the problems students will have with the material. A parent can predict both the tone and the content of a child's impending conversation simply from the way the door slams after school.

It's not magic—it's understanding that grows from wisdom and love—the same wisdom and love, on a smaller scale, that God has for his own children. He knows us and our needs. This doesn't make the asking less necessary—it only gives us more confidence that the One who knows us so well will give us exactly the answer we need.

Lord, today I come to you with my
greatest needs, in confidence and trust.

Breaking down walls with love

I have given you a model to follow, so that as
I have done for you, you should also do.

JOHN 13:15

Mary Jo Copeland is the founder of Sharing and Caring Hands, a tremendously effective outreach to the poor in Minneapolis. The group runs shelters and transitional homes, day programs for teens and children, and is generally known for being there to meet the needs of the poor, at any time. Every evening, Mary Jo ends the workday by taking out basins, filling them with warm water, and then washing the feet of at least twelve people. She says that in washing feet, she is trying to share with the poor the reality of their own dignity as children of God.

These days are all about love. What Jesus has done for the disciples, he tells them, they are called to do for others. And what is that? It seems it might be to love, which is far more than kindness or good-feeling. Jesus, Son of God, reaches out through washing feet, through the sharing of his own Body and Blood, breaking down walls with love.

Jesus, Master, lead me
in your way of service and love.

Groping my way toward God

These were their thoughts, but they erred;
for their wickedness blinded them.

WISDOM 2:21

In a large city recently for one convention, I found myself in the midst of another that was meeting at my hotel: the National Federation for the Blind. To be surrounded by literally thousands of people without sight was a fascinating, revealing experience. I was very interested in their ways of coping with the world: the tools they needed, the adjustments they made, the occasional help they required of others.

I have my physical sight, but I'm aware of other types of blindness in my own life. I know that, as the author of Wisdom writes, my sinfulness can blind me. When I hold back from God, I have a hard time seeing the power and possibility of choosing good or the goodness and full humanity of others. I can be deceived into misinterpreting the shadows around me, coming to believe that what the world offers will bring me lasting happiness.

That's why I need to accept the reality of my own lack of perfect sight and be willing to accept the help, insight, and wisdom of others so that I might make my way toward deeper love of God—despite the obstacles.

Lord, help me find my way to you.

Love means sacrificing our wills

*"…to love your neighbor as yourself" is worth more
than all burnt offerings and sacrifices.*

MARK 12:33

My daughter, who is thirteen, is just terribly anxious that I understand how ready she is to baby-sit her little brother, who is three.

However, her unreadiness is regularly played out in a scene like this: The two of them start to play, and within minutes there's an argument. My daughter's trying to get her brother to play a certain way, and he, being as reflexively stubborn as she, refuses. He's got his own thing going on. But for some reason, she persists, insisting that things have to be done her way. All this with a three-year-old.

I try to point out to her that this is silly; what's more, it isn't love. The scribe speaking with Jesus is correct in saying that loving others is what God wants of us above all else, including material sacrifices.

What we often forget is that love is a sacrifice. As my daughter's experience shows in such a small way, real love can be an even more difficult sacrifice than merely external expressions, for real love involves a sacrifice of our wills, our own pleasure, and our own egos.

Jesus, form me in your sacrificial love.

32

Forgiveness is at the core of faith

Then Peter approaching asked him, "Lord, if my brother sins against me, how often must I forgive him? As many as seven times?"

MATTHEW 18:21

The arguments we can offer against forgiveness all crumble under the force of Jesus' words. And not only his words: Most of us have crucifixes in our houses, and some of us wear them around our necks, day and night. That figure on the cross hangs, not just as a witness to suffering and love, but to forgiveness. "Father, forgive them," Jesus said from the cross, and those who remembered his words did so, I imagine, because they understood they were directed not just at those who had physically pounded the nails, but at everyone and everything about a broken world that had put him on that cross.

Why forgive? Think of the arguments we offer against forgiveness. What do they have to do with Jesus? Anything at all?

Jesus, let your forgiveness
and mercy flow through me,
no matter what the cost.

A gift for the young

However, take care and be earnestly on your guard not to forget the things which your own eyes have seen, nor let them slip from your memory as long as you live, but teach them to your children...

DEUTERONOMY 4:9

When I was a classroom teacher, I noticed that the more I taught something, the better I learned it. Not rocket science, I suppose, but there it is. I learned a lot in college—at least I thought I did. But none of it has stuck quite as well as the material I had to teach to others, even just once or twice.

Many of the reasons to share our wisdom with the young are so obvious it seems silly to repeat them. But perhaps this reason might give new food for thought: Remembering where we have been, what we have learned and what God has done for us is a gift for the young, but is also a gift to ourselves. In the telling, the teaching, the sharing, we learn it all again. It becomes even more firmly imprinted on our hearts, and harder to forget when we are tempted, however we may be tempted, to do so.

Lord, teach me as I share
your love with others.

Refusing to acknowledge God's mercy

*Then Peter approaching asked him,
"Lord, if my brother sins against me, how often must
I forgive him? As many as seven times?" Jesus answered,
"I say to you, not seven times but seventy-seven times."*

MATTHEW 18:21-22

Forgiving our brothers and sisters is one thing. Forgiving ourselves is another, isn't it? Now, I'm not trying to dilute Jesus' primary message here, but I have to say that when I think about my own life and some others whom I know well, forgiveness of ourselves seems to be a huge obstacle in spiritual growth.

Forgiving oneself isn't just an egocentric exercise either, because truth be told, it all comes down this: accepting the fact that God has forgiven me. Refusing to acknowledge mercy can be just as devastating as refusing to acknowledge sin, can't it? File them both under "I know better than God."

How many times? Seventy-seven, that is, without end. God's mercy, working through my life, without end. Whether I think I deserve it or not.

Father, help me let go of my pride and allow your mercy to flourish in my life.

An honored past, a rich present

*It was because the Lord loved you and because of his fidelity
to the oath he had sworn to your fathers, that he brought you
out with his strong hand from the place of slavery...*

DEUTERONOMY 7:8

I was unloading a crate of library books from the car when an
older gentleman appeared on my driveway. After saying hello, he
said, "My dad built this house."

He and his wife were in town for a reunion. As we walked
through the house, he pointed out inventive features his father
had included and told my surprised first-grader that, as a boy, he
had gone to the same school he attends now.

Knowing a bit more of the history of the house in which we
live, and the heart that had gone into its making, made me care
more for it in the present.

Moses reminded the people of Israel of their history—that
they were God's beloved children. It was a reminder they needed
again and again as they faced suffering and profound questions.
We're called to live in the now, certainly, but the present is so
much richer when we understand and honor the past.

Lord God, I thank you
for all you have done for me.

God is near in life—and death

The Lord is with me to the end.

PSALM 138:8

A little more than two years ago, my mother lay dying, and there was no way I—her only child—could be there with her. I was nine months pregnant, due any day, and a six-hour car trip away. So I couldn't go.

I was kept informed by my father, but it was not the same as being there. My mother was beyond coherent communication herself, so I could hear how she was, but I couldn't see, couldn't be there to do whatever it was I could have done.

What frustrated me most was that, as much as those around her cared for her, no one shared her faith—our faith. I sensed from what I was being told that there was a spiritual component to my mother's suffering, something that no one there could really deal with, and that I might have been able to assuage, just a little bit. Perhaps.

But faith tells me that the most important One of all was there, all the time. I trust that to be true. For my mother. For me. Even when I think I am suffering alone.

Lord, deepen my awareness
of your presence here.

First seek God, then "inner peace"

For you know the gracious act of our Lord Jesus Christ,
that for your sake he became poor although he was rich,
so that by his poverty you might become rich.

2 CORINTHIANS 8:9

I'm starting to wonder about the air I breath. The spiritual air, that is, the air that's drifting around my culture's definition of what the spiritual life is all about. Because in that air is an assumption that my spiritual life is essentially about me: about finding peace, a space where I feel accepted and comfortable.

But when I actually go back to the sources—to, say, Paul writing here to the Christians in Corinth to encourage them to pour out more of themselves in love, because their redemption came as Christ poured himself out for them—I have to think again. It almost seems to be a different language sometimes.

Joy and peace are the fruit of this journey, but the name of the journey might be something different from what some of us think. It might not be so much, "The way to inner peace," but simply, "Discipleship."

Lord Jesus, fill me with your love,
so that I might share it with others.

Learning to trust

Happy are those who fear the Lord...
PSALM 112:1

Over the past month, I've done a bit of flying. More, in fact, than I've done in the previous ten years put together.

It is not exactly my favorite mode of travel. Sure, I appreciate the speed, but I will admit that I'm not exactly fearless up there. When those engines shift on ascent, there's turbulence, or the plane starts rocking on descent—I don't like it at all.

Things have changed just a bit from the past, though. In previous years, when those moments arrived, I'd be praying, sort of frantically, to stay safe. It's different now. I'm still not completely at peace, and I sure would like to stay physically alive, but whether it be age or just the tiniest bit more faith, I find my heart to be more tranquil because somehow, somewhere, I've learned to trust. No matter what will happen, I'll trust the Lord.

Lord, help me trust in
your loving care for me.

Easter to Pentecost

To see thee more clearly

*As a result of this, many [of] his disciples returned to
their former way of life and no longer accompanied him.*

JOHN 6:66

On a recent weekend, members of my family all spotted famous
people. My son the film nut saw a well-known director. My
sports nut son saw a pro basketball great. And my political science dad saw a former U.S. senator in an airport. What struck
me was that each of these guys saw folks involved with their
main passions in life. That's who was in their framework, their
line of sight.

I wondered. I have my paradigms, my ways of seeing. Firmly
ensconced in that box...what might I be missing? Jesus de-
scribed himself as the Bread of life. He said that eating his flesh
and drinking his blood brought eternal life. It was too much for
some. It was absolutely outside what they were used to seeing
and thinking. So they walked away.

What did they lose because of what they were unwilling to
even try to see?

Jesus, widen my vision
to see you more clearly.

How to pray, how to live

This is how you are to pray:
Our Father in heaven,
hallowed be your name...
MATTHEW 6:9

In any bookstore or library, shelves are filled with books about prayer: how to pray, how to get the most out of prayer, how to have a fulfilling spiritual life. We all have a lot of questions about this most important part of life. Good for us that Jesus has already answered them—briefly and simply.

For these words—what we call the Lord's Prayer— aren't just phrases for us to repeat in our own prayer. They are just what Jesus says: a model for how to pray.

And notice who's front and center: is it me and my problems? My hard decisions and regrets? Is this the time for trying to convince God to be reasonable and see things my way?

It's really no surprise. Jesus' lesson in prayer begins with acknowledging and praising God and then praying that God's will be done—

That's how to pray, but even more, how to live.

Our Father, who art in heaven...

You...food...love

*While they were still incredulous for joy and were amazed,
[Jesus] asked them, "Have you anything here to eat?" They gave
him a piece of baked fish; he took it and ate it in front of them.*

LUKE 24:41-43

Old habits die hard—habits like a mother's desire to care for
a child. So even though after a long day at school and theater
rehearsal, my seventeen-year-old daughter could throw her own
dinner together while I took care of other things, I find myself
insisting on getting her food.

There's no nobility on my part. There's just a primeval satisfaction involved in setting down a plate of food in front of your
tired, hungry, and frustrated child. There is not much you can
do for her. But you can do this. Your presence, plus food, equals
love.

Jesus, risen from the dead, spoke to his amazed disciples. He
showed them his wounds. And then, in utter, everyday simplicity, he asked them for something to eat. His presence, plus food,
equals love.

Risen Lord, I rejoice in your love.

Jesus is "married" to the Church

I also saw the holy city, a new Jerusalem,
coming down out of heaven from God,
prepared as a bride adorned for her husband.

REVELATION 21:2

Over the past few years, the novel and film *The Da Vinci Code* fueled a lot of questions. One that many people found particularly interesting was whether Jesus and Mary Magdalene could have indeed, as the novel so confidently proclaimed, been married.

Well, of course not—for reasons too many to name here—except for one: Jesus is, indeed, "married" to the Church. It's an ancient image, and one that's echoed in this passage from Revelation, wherein the new Jerusalem, the Church, arrayed as a bride, approaches her Lord. Near the end of the book, the image recurs as the reader is invited to join this great vision: "The Spirit and the bride say, 'Come'" (Revelation 22:17). Jesus' mission is redemptive and cosmic, his presence faithful, loving, and intimate, like a spouse, sacrificing all for his beloved—us.

Jesus, I rejoice in your
deep and faithful love.

Beyond good intentions

*Jesus looked at them and said, "For human beings
it is impossible, but not for God. All things are possible for God."*

MARK 10:27

The three-year-old gets corrected several times a day. Lately, he
has developed a new response. He insists, "I don't want to be
bad!" Over and over, he'll say it, whining or bellowing, depend-
ing on the urgency of the moment. It's either "I don't want to be
bad!" or "I want to be good!"

Our reflexive response is almost always, "Then be good..." To
which he invariably responds, "I don't want to be bad!" without
any sense that words are not going to change anything.

How often am I just like the toddler? I say that I really should
give myself more fully to the Lord. Honestly, I would really like
to. I want to be good! But the prospect of suffering for the sake
of love seems too much to bear. How can I ever get beyond the
words and good intentions? It seems impossible... But is it?

Lord Jesus, fill me
and strengthen me.

No need to "dice up religion"

*A woman named Lydia… listened, and the Lord opened
her heart to pay attention to what Paul was saying.*

ACTS 16:14

On a recent trip in the car, my husband chanced upon a radio discussion of religious matters. The host, guest, and callers were arguing about the fate of the Good Thief, each side appealing to all types of arcane reasons why they were correct in their view of how the thief could have been saved. Jesus' promise to the thief seemed to weigh little in the discussion.

Both my husband and I thought the same thing at the same time: "This is why people get turned off by religion." The temptation to use our God-given minds to dice up religious matters into tiny points of argumentation seems almost irresistible.

But resist we must, don't you think? Perhaps one of the best ways to do so is to look at the experiences of the converts in Acts like Lydia. How much of our faith struggles come from forgetting their example and thinking that there must be a better way than simply listening and responding in love and openness?

Lord, open my heart to
your Word and give me the
patience to pay attention.

Staying open to the unexpected

Now there was an Ethiopian eunuch, a court official....
Seated in his chariot, he was reading the prophet Isaiah.

ACTS 8:27-28

At first glance, it just seems odd. Odd that on the road from Jerusalem, Philip would meet the official in charge of the Ethiopian court treasury reading the Hebrew Scriptures, and, odder still, he would end up baptizing him.

There are times at which I get far too settled in my own ways of seeing things. I'm so absorbed in the task of figuring out God's ways in my own life and habits that I'm tempted to look at others and see nothing or no one worth noting, instead of my brothers and sisters on the same journey as I am, with the same God moving in their hearts.

What am I missing when I close myself off from the unexpected? Who else is journeying down the road?

Jesus, open my eyes to the reality
of your love for every person.

Living in truth brings lasting joy

But they cried out in a loud voice,
covered their ears, and rushed upon him together.

ACTS 7:57

Saint Stephen is under attack here, and sadly enough, it is religious leaders who have covered their ears, unwilling to be confronted by truth.

Facing the truth can be painful, there's no doubt. There are times at which the phone rings, and I dread picking it up because I know it's one of my young adult sons, deep in a mess I can't fix. Or I see the look on my daughter's face when she comes home from school, and I think, "I can't. I can't hear about what mean girls have done to you today. It hurts too much and makes me too angry. Can't we just pretend?"

No, we can't. And if we're honest, we'll admit that we don't want to pretend. We know that the only real, lasting joy is in living in the truth.

Lord, give me the courage
to face a painful truth today.

50

Jesus, the one focus of faith

Repent and be baptized, every one of you, in the
name of Jesus Christ for the forgiveness of your sins;
and you will receive the gift of the Holy Spirit.

ACTS 2:38

Over the years, I've thought of many reasons to stick to my Christian faith, and I've heard a good many others: believing in something beyond ourselves is good; there's a rich, interesting, life-affirming tradition in Christianity; what Christianity teaches is good for morals, good for raising children. My local faith community is so welcoming, like a family, and I get so much out of my involvement in its activities, as do my kids, I can't imagine not going to church. It's such a part of my life, of my routine, my week, my Sunday. It's just part of who I am and what I do.

These might be good reasons, but they aren't mentioned when I read the accounts of those who responded to the earliest preaching of the apostles. Rather, the focus is precise, exact, and centered in one place: the salvation and mercy found in Jesus.

All of those other graces I experience are certainly the fruit of this faith, but these Easter days hold Jesus firmly before me as the root of it all.

Risen Jesus, fill my life with
your mercy, love, and hope.

Listen carefully to know God's will

*They traveled through the Phrygian and Galatian territory
because they had been prevented by the holy Spirit from
preaching the message in the province of Asia.*

ACTS 16:6

How mysterious are the promptings of the Spirit! This passage
has no explanation of what exactly Paul and Timothy experienced. What happened that prevented them from going to Asia?
How did they know it was the Spirit?

The simple answer, I suppose, would be that if they were prevented from going, that was God's will. This passage is directly
followed by another indicating that the "Spirit of Jesus" prevented them from going in another direction, and the end result was
that the missionaries changed course and headed for Europe,
where they fruitfully preached the Gospel.

It is a strong reminder that what we are about is God's will,
not ours. Sometimes that will is blindingly clear, other times
more difficult to discern. Sometimes it's about staying in the
place where we're authentically at peace; other times it involves
something completely unexpected and initially frustrating. All
God asks is that we listen—and respond.

Lord, quiet my desires
so I can listen to your Spirit.

Sleeping like a baby

Remain in me, as I remain in you. Just as a branch cannot bear fruit on its own unless it remains on the vine, so neither can you unless you remain in me.

JOHN 15:4

My babies don't sleep in the same bed with me all the time, but often enough, they do. It's not a political point with me, as it is for some, but more a factor of laziness than anything else.

In parenting young babies, though, I have discovered something: they do, in fact, sleep better when they're with me. When they wake, as babies do, they open their eyes and see, not bars on a crib, but the face they know best. And most of the time, they close their eyes and go right back to sleep without a peep, secure in my presence.

Remaining attached to Jesus, I feel the same way. When I have pushed him away, into another room of my life, life takes on a different shape. It is a less certain place. But opening my eyes and remembering to whom I am attached, by his love, I feel safe, and paradoxically, more free to be myself.

Jesus, I cling to you in love.

When appearances deceive

When [Paul] arrived in Jerusalem he tried to
join the disciples, but they were all afraid of him...
ACTS 9:26

Who could blame them for being afraid of Saul? After all, to them, he was their persecutor, the farthest thing from a disciple. How could they trust him? Why should they trust him?

I remember the first time I had my expectations of another person completely confounded. It was a college professor whose severe appearance—fierce eyes and a Lincoln-type beard—and strict demeanor terrified me, despite the distance between his podium and my desk. A point came, however, when I had to go speak with him. I had no choice. And of course, the person I encountered was unfailingly kind and helpful. Not a bit the monster I had expected.

Those disciples had far more reason than I to be cautious. Excellent reason, in fact. But the incident shows once more how important it is to keep hearts and minds open, willing to be surprised by others—and by the God who can transform the hardest heart.

God, give me the grace to be open
to the surprising ways you can
change hearts—even mine.

Resurrection faith

For if we believe that Jesus died and rose, so too will God,
through Jesus, bring with him those who have fallen asleep.
1 THESSALONIANS 4:14

I have to admit that I am not all that confident about death yet.
In my head, I've got it, but so many times my spirit falters, as I
glance over obituaries, drive by cemeteries, or contemplate the
strange but true fact that in a hundred years, someone will be
reading the happenings of my time in the same way I read the
events of a century ago—as history.

So at those times, I must, if I'm to remain sane, retrieve my
faith from my head and confront it with my whole life this time.
Am I really the Christian I claim to be? Really the disciple? Yes?
Well then that means that I believe that Jesus rose from the
dead—and I do—and that when I close my eyes that last time,
he'll come.

Sometimes it's an easy bridge to cross, sometimes it's harder.
But fastening my eyes and heart on him, I cross.

Jesus, fill my heart with
hope in your promise.

"To Jerusalem's closed door we go"

Because there arose no little dissension and debate by Paul and Barnabas with them, it was decided that Paul, Barnabas, and some of the others should go up to Jerusalem...about this question.

ACTS 15:2

When my daughter and I have disagreed, I approach her closed door and sometimes just wish that I could let it stay closed, that I wouldn't have to knock, encounter whatever mood she has ready for me, and slowly but surely work through it all to the other side. Frankly, I'd rather not do it sometimes. I'd rather just go back downstairs and lose myself in a book.

But I can't. The temptation is strong to pretend disagreement doesn't exist, to try to push it in the background, to simply avoid the tough work of reconciliation and understanding.

These early Christians faced an incredibly deep disagreement: the relationship of gentile Christians to Jewish Law. People on both sides had very strong feelings, and knew that the way to a solution would require sacrifice. But shared faith in Christ is real faith, and it can't pretend. So up to Jerusalem—or up to that closed door—we go.

Spirit of God, bring peace and understanding to my relationships.

Festivals

Generosity is the heart of faith

ST. NICHOLAS

Great crowds came to him, having with them the lame,
the blind, the deformed, the mute, and many others.
They placed them at his feet, and he cured them.

MATTHEW 15:30

I never fail to be amazed by the number of people who harbor the strong belief that this Christianity business is all about rules and restrictions. Of course, some of us who should know better probably still feel that way at times. At times.

But when we actually enter into the life of Jesus and his disciples over the centuries, what strikes us is not rules, but an overflow of lavish, extravagant love, shared with all. God's passion to reknit his broken creation is expressed in the touch of Jesus—himself the greatest gift, born in weakness, ready to embrace us if we choose.

The legends of St. Nicholas reflect this. Today we remember this kind bishop for his generosity to the poor and gift of self for the sake of his people—which, if you think about it, is a part of the story of most of the saints we honor.

In this season of gifts, I'm glad to be reminded that generosity is at the heart of faith, beginning with the gift of Jesus.

Clearing away the obstacles

IMMACULATE CONCEPTION

Hail, favored one! The Lord is with you.
LUKE 1:28

We echo the angel's words to Mary all the time, although in slightly different language. Hail Mary, full of grace, we say. Or, in that concise elegance of Latin, *Ave Maria, gratia plena.* And what does that mean?

Mary's "yes" is not just about her and God. It's about all of us—the whole, winding, messy journey of humanity. She's giving herself over completely to God for his loving purposes.

It's always made sense to me that God would prepare her from the beginning for this. As Pope Benedict once wrote, "Her life is such that she is a place for God." Mary couldn't do that alone. She couldn't do that at all. Only God can clear out the obstacles, which he did for Mary from her conception. And which he does within us, too, beginning with the waters of baptism and continuing, in ways large and small throughout our lives, with each "yes" we offer him.

Hail Mary, full of grace,
the Lord is with you...

Prenatal premonition

VISITATION OF THE VIRGIN MARY

*When Elizabeth heard Mary's greeting, the infant leaped
in her womb, and Elizabeth, filled with the holy Spirit,
cried out in a loud voice and said, "Most blessed are you
among women, and blessed is the fruit of your womb."*

LUKE 1:41-42

We were all unborn children once, and in that warm darkness
we all grew, learned, and, yes, listened. Any pregnant woman will
tell you of the feeling she has, perhaps rooted partly in intuition
and partly in hopeful, expectant imagination, that even within
the womb, her child had a mind of its own. When she rests,
the baby awakes and does somersaults. When, heavily pregnant,
she tries to move a sharp knee or elbow away from her ribs, she
might just feel a push back in silent, stubborn retort.

It is the place where our lives of discernment began, where
we learn for the first time, wordlessly, important truths about
love, dependence, simplicity, and peace. It has always intrigued
and awed me that the first person to recognize Jesus as Lord was
an unborn child.

Jesus, I rejoice in your
presence in my life.

Living by God's definitions

ST. POLYCARP

This, rather, is the fasting that I wish...
Sharing your bread with the hungry,
sheltering the oppressed and the homeless...
ISAIAH 58:6, 7

Saint Polycarp was a bishop who was martyred in the second century, and there's one part of his story that's particularly awesome, as the kids like to say.

Brought into the arena where the pyre was being prepared, the bishop was ordered to make this statement: "Away with the atheists!" Meaning, of course, the "atheist" Christians, who didn't believe in the Roman gods or the Imperial divinity.

So Polycarp said it. But he turned the words on their head, gazing boldly at the gathered crowd, gazing to heaven and saying those words: "Away with the atheists."

Not exactly what the authorities hoped.

So much hangs on definitions, doesn't it? It seems to me that part of being a Christian involves trying to live by God's definitions, not the world's. Polycarp gives us a pithy example, and so does the prophet Isaiah. What am I doing when I "fast"? Is this what God means? What about when I "love?" Am I loving by my own standards or by God's?

Loving God, I seek to live in your Word.

"Seventy-seven times"

ST. PATRICK

Then Peter approaching asked him, "Lord, if my brother sins against me, how often must I forgive him? As many as seven times?" Jesus answered, "I say to you, not seven times, but seventy-seven times."

MATTHEW 18:21-22

"She's dead to me." That catchphrase sums up a popular attitude towards hurting and forgiveness, doesn't it? But consider instead, St. Patrick. When he was a boy, Patrick was kidnapped from his home in Britain by Irish raiders. Years later, he discerned a call to preach the gospel and bring the truth of Jesus Christ…to the Irish. The very people who had kidnapped and enslaved him. Forgiveness, personified.

What is it that makes this kind of forgiveness possible? Nothing but the grace of God, of course, "grace" being the loving presence of God. Patrick knew how profound his captors' need for Christ was. He knew that better than anyone else, in fact. And so, seeing them with the loving eyes of God, he forgave. Then, just as Jesus did, he gave his life to those who had harmed him. Not exactly dead to him—the opposite, in fact: potentially fully alive, in Christ!

Lord Jesus, fill me
with the grace to forgive.

Listening to God's whispers

ST. JOSEPH

Behold, the angel of the Lord appeared to him in a dream.
MATTHEW 1:20

When Pope Benedict came to the United States, he spoke to many groups in many different venues. One of the most memorable was the gathering with youth at St. Joseph's Seminary in Dunwoodie, New York. It was memorable in the way these events always are—the young responding enthusiastically to words of wisdom from the Holy Father and he, in turn, enlivened by their energy.

But it was also memorable to me for one specific phrase in the pope's talk. It's something I haven't been able to forget. At one point, in calling the young people to involve God in their life choices, he simply asked, "What is God whispering to you?"

What an appropriate place to plant such a seed—a place named after St. Joseph who overcame fear and confusion because he responded in faith to the whisperings of God through a dream.

What is God whispering to you?

Lord, I still whisper to
myself and listen to you.

Joy that lasts

TRANSFIGURATION OF THE LORD

Lord, it is good that we are here. If you wish, I will make three tents here, one for you, one for Moses, and one for Elijah.
MATTHEW 17:4

Of course, Peter could do no such thing. Those moments in which we experience the deep, abiding, peace-filled presence of the Lord are certainly real, but they can't be packaged.

When I hold my little children in my arms, I can't get enough of their softness and openhearted hugs. But at other times, I weary of their dependence.

On the other hand, my older children are independent, which carries its own kind of satisfaction. But along with that goes the end of the sweetness of early childhood, and even their daily presence in my life.

I can't have it all right now. Life's joys come and go and even seem at odds with each other at times. They can't be contained.

But even in this, I can see a hint of the future. In heaven, all the joys I so briefly glimpse here will be gathered up and be transfigured into the eternal, glorious presence of Love that never ends.

Lord, I take joy in my journey
to eternal life with you.

Praying for ones who seem lost

ST. MONICA

Where can I hide from your spirit?
from your presence where can I flee?

PSALM 139:7

One does not need to be a parent to sympathize with the love that drove St. Monica, mother of St. Augustine. Following her brilliant, sometimes misguided son around the Mediterranean, she would not relent, would not stop praying that he would one day open his heart to God.

All of us probably have at least one person in our lives who pierces our heart the same way St. Augustine did Monica's. We watch a sibling, cousin, or even parent struggle with faith, and we can't help but worry and pray. A friend takes a path that seems wrong, and we are powerless to stop him or her. We do all we can to help those dearest to us experience the love and mercy of God, but still, they seem lost in sadness, untethered from hope.

The psalmist helps us put our efforts in the proper perspective. Like St. Monica, we should never stop praying, but we should also recognize that those we love are indeed on their own journeys, and even though it's hard to see, on that journey, they are not alone.

Lord, today I pray for those who seem lost.
Assure them of your presence and love.

Hope helps us bear heavy loads

ALL SAINTS

They stood before the throne and before the Lamb,
wearing white robes and holding palm branches in their hands.

REVELATION 7:9

I was cleaning out the basement the other day, accompanied by the ever-helpful two-year-old. One of the things I found was the large baby back carrier we'd carried him in a few times in some travels the year before. His eyes lit up in recognition when he saw it. "Oh yeah!" he chirped, "That can wear me!" What he meant, of course, was that he was "worn" by mommy or daddy in the carrier. Typically ingenious, totally rational toddler logic.

In this passage from Revelation, we meet the saints, wearing white robes. We wore those white robes at our baptisms, signs of our new identity, being new creations in Christ. We wear the robes still, symbolically, because we are still on that disciple's journey. There were moments in those walks through big cities when my son got very, very heavy on my back. Perhaps we feel the same way about that identity as a disciple—it is heavier than we expected at times. But we continue on the journey, knowing that what we wear—inside and out—is a sign of hope.

Jesus, I praise you
with the saints in heaven.

67

Facing darkness

ST. STEPHEN

As they were stoning Stephen, he called out,
"Lord Jesus, receive my spirit."
ACTS 7:59

Yesterday, Christmas, was all about a baby and joyous songs of praise. Today, a man is crushed to death under the weight of hurtling stones. How strange that the Feast of St. Stephen, the first Christian martyr, directly follows the celebration of the Nativity. How strange, but how appropriate.

For even in the stories of Jesus' birth and infancy, we hear intimations of what is to come. The Good News drives Herod into a fit of murderous rage. Mary must absorb the message that because of this child, a sword will pierce her heart. John's gospel tells us the Word is a light sent to illuminate darkness. Yesterday, we celebrated the light. Today, without even a chance to take a breath, we confront the darkness.

We may be tempted to simply turn away. But Stephen's story calls us back. It calls us back to the truth that when we accept the Child, we accept all that he is: not aloof, but fully immersed in the world with all of its joy and risk. And where he goes, we, like Stephen, can bravely follow in love.

Lord, fill my heart with the
courage to love as you do.

Guarding the innocent from harm

THE HOLY INNOCENTS

Joseph rose and took the child and his mother
by night and departed for Egypt.

MATTHEW 2:14

As he obeyed God's message to him through a dream, Joseph was able to protect those in his care. All around me, the innocent are threatened by so much. Abortion, hunger, abuse, and poverty take their toll. Quietly, alone, or as part of a suffering nation, the innocent suffer.

At the same time, in dreams and beyond, I think I, too, hear a message. I know what God wants—it's no mystery. I know that just as he worked through Joseph, God can and wants to work through me to guard the innocent from harm, in whatever small or great way I can.

Joseph listened and obeyed. Do I listen? Or would I rather just change the channel and forget?

Lord, open my heart to the
cries of the innocent.

Story line

STS. PETER AND PAUL

For I am already being poured out like a libation, and the
time of my departure is at hand. I have competed well;
I have finished the race; I have kept the faith.

2 TIMOTHY 4:6-7

These days, it is rather fashionable to speak of faith and religion in terms of "story." The idea is that we structure our faith around a story that is meaningful to us. For some, it doesn't matter if it's actually true or not—what matters is the comfort we find in the story.

I don't know about you, but I don't find that notion very comforting at all.

I also doubt that this is what Paul is talking about when he writes these words, probably in a period between imprisonment and execution.

Peter's and Paul's faith wasn't in an idea or a story that helped them make sense of life. It was in a person—Jesus Christ, the one who loved, reconciled, sacrificed, and opened our broken lives to the transforming love of God. To share him with the world: that's a race worth running, no matter what the cost.

Jesus, strengthen me to live for you and
share your Good News with others.

A friend in need is a friend indeed

ST. FRANCIS XAVIER

Without cost you have received; without cost you are to give.

MATTHEW 10:8

Far away from home in the Midwest, we were attending Mass at San Xavier del Bac, an old mission church south of Tucson, Arizona. Built in the 18th century and in constant use since then, the church was packed with Native American and Hispanic parishioners and tourists. Before and after Mass, a line formed and crept toward the side in front of the sanctuary. There, in a glass casket open on the side, lay a mannequin of St. Francis Xavier.

As they approached, pilgrims laid a hand or two on the statue. Some slipped a hand under the neck and lifted it slightly. I was told later that if the statue offered little or no resistance, the petitioner's prayer would be answered.

Who knows about that? What I did know about, once again, was the power of saints. A man born long ago who gave his life for God and God's children, a missionary of God's love, was being treated as a friend in need centuries later, all under the watchful eyes of angels dancing on the ceiling.

Lord, fill me with your love,
so that I might share it, too.

Ordinary
Time

God "needs" our prayers

While the two men walked on farther toward Sodom, the Lord
remained standing before Abraham. Then Abraham drew nearer to
him and said: "Will you sweep away the innocent with the guilty?"

GENESIS 18:22-23

Prayer can be a puzzle. More people than you might think are
tripped up by that most common of prayers: prayers of supplication or petition. We wonder and raise a score of questions: How
can this even be necessary? Why does God need me and my
prayers to get things done? Isn't such prayer just for children?

C.S. Lewis helpfully pointed out that we might as well ask
why God needs us at all—for anything. For some reason, some
mysterious reason, human creatures are a part of his plan, part of
how he gets things done. And prayer is a part of that. Prayer in
all forms, and most especially supplication.

Jesus himself told parables and gave advice about praying for
our needs and the needs of others. And here in Genesis, we find
this most amazing story, with theological mysteries that no one
has ever completely unpacked: God's actions being influenced
by the prayer, the begging, the questions of Abraham.

And in the midst of this mystery—we pray.

Lord, I present my needs to you.
Hear me!

Be patient in assessing net profit

The kingdom of heaven is like a net thrown into the sea, which collects fish of every kind. When it is full they haul it ashore and sit down to put what is good into buckets. What is bad they throw away.

MATTHEW 13:47-48

Rome is a city of contradictions: from narrow streets arise huge, gorgeous churches filled with angels and saints, many of them constructed by the most profligate of sinners, clerical and lay alike. How it all fits together makes your head spin. The old story—good coming from less-than-good—is also a new story. When I trace the events of my life, every step seems just as confused as those elaborate Roman churches. Good comes from evil, tragedy, and terrible mistakes. Following what seem like positive promptings, I go astray in an uncritical haze of good intentions.

Jesus' parable reminds me to be careful and patient—with myself and especially others. I can't ever stop pursuing holiness and discerning the promptings of the Spirit, but I can't despair either. God can bring good out of anything; I have to be careful not to judge where others will end up once the net is hauled ashore. The Fisherman is in charge of that.

Holy Spirit, help me see
your presence, even in the darkness.

A year of rest

*This fiftieth year you shall make sacred by proclaiming liberty
in the land for all its inhabitants. It shall be a jubilee for you,
when every one of you shall return to his own property,
every one to his own family estate.*

LEVITICUS 25:10

In this astonishing passage from the Hebrew Scriptures, we read of liberation: it was called the Year of Jubilee. Every fifty years, the people of Israel let the land—God's land—observe a Sabbath rest. They were to absolve debts, free slaves, and return to their family's land. It was, in spirit, a return to Eden, to God's intentions for his creation and his children.

What would a jubilee, a year of redemption, mean for you? From what debts would you be freed? What impulses, habits, and worldly concerns that now enslave you would disappear? Who is waiting at home for you? Whom are you ready to embrace once again?

There's no reason to wait, no calendars to flip, no watches to check. Jesus' invitation is always open: "Come to me, all you who labor and are burdened, and I will give you rest" (Matthew 11:28).

In Jesus, every moment is a Year of Jubilee.

Jesus, I give you what burdens me,
trusting you will give me rest.

"There's life at the end"

We know that all creation is groaning
in labor pains even until now.
ROMANS 8:22

Do you want to know about labor pains? Allow me: no matter how much she has prepared, no matter how many times she has done it before, a woman in labor, at some time or another, confronts the rather strong feeling that things are way out of control. Your body seems to be doing its own thing, and the best you can do is hang on for dear life and try, try to keep your inner gaze focused on the other dear life within that is straining towards light, inching towards your arms.

It seems like a confusing, crazy mess. But it's not. There's a reason for every contraction, strain, and pain. And there's life at the end.

As Paul notes in this wise passage from Romans, this is also the world's journey. It strains, it labors, and there are times— so much time—that the strain of the laboring overwhelms and seems to take on a life of its own with no purpose that we can see. Paul assures us that the purpose may be difficult to see, but the victory of Jesus reveals to us that at the end of this kind of laboring, too, there is life.

Lord, may I keep my faith in you
in the midst of life's difficulties.

78

Prayer, public and private

When you pray, do not be like the hypocrites, who love to stand and pray in the synagogues and on street corners so that others may see them....When you pray, go to your inner room, close the door, and pray to your Father in secret.

MATTHEW 6:5-6

I rather think most of us aren't too disturbed by Jesus' admonition not to take pleasure in praying in public. After all, who among us enthusiastically leaps at the chance to lead prayer before a meeting or at a big meal? Yes, prayer in private is just the thing.

Even so, perhaps there's something in Jesus' words for the quiet ones among us. Remember, he always challenges us to focus on our motives. The point of these words isn't so much the fact of praying in public, but the motivation for doing so. Otherwise, how could we worship together at all?

So what do I hear in Jesus' words to me today? Perhaps to be careful that my prayer doesn't become rote or simply to fulfill a duty. Or that I think God needs to hear me say a lot or do complicated feats of prayer in order to tend to me.

No, even in private, Jesus' words challenge me to go deeper, to trust, and to quietly listen.

Loving Father, I come to you
in love and trust.

Acting on an impulse

As they traveled along the road they came to some water,
and the eunuch said, "Look, there is water.
What is to prevent my being baptized?"

ACTS 8:36

What, indeed, prevents me? Not from being baptized (since that happened long ago), but from really opening myself to the grace of that baptism and growing in my faith?

Pride? Fear of losing some part of my life I believe is essential? A hesitancy to give up control? A fear of what others might say or think? Claims that I'm too busy, that I'm fine just as I am?

The Ethiopian eunuch was moved by the Spirit. He didn't push that nudge aside, ignore it, or try to argue it away. I have to wonder about the nudges I have felt today. What is to prevent me from listening and acting on them?

Lord, break down the obstacles
I've put up to your presence.

"Give to everyone who asks"

*Give to everyone who asks of you, and from the one
who takes what is yours do not demand it back.*

LUKE 6:30

When we traveled to Rome last year, one of my major worries
was how to deal with the masses of beggars it was rumored we
would encounter. I was mostly concerned for my sensitive teen
daughter's sake. She needed to know that much of what she
would see would be acting, a ruse for thievery or simply a cre-
ative form of employment.

But over the week we were there, despite my resolve, a battle
raged within my own heart. The women sitting at the church
doors? The handicapped guy scooting around in Campo di
Fiore? The girls with the babies? Was I being scammed? If I
gave, would I be contributing to the problem of exploitation of
these women and children?

"Put your Euros in the church poor boxes," everyone said.
"The churches know who and how to help." And we did that.
But still the questions haunted at every church door where a real
person sat, holding a cup, a baby, or both. What am I holding
on to?

Lord, grant me a generous
and discerning heart.

The unwelcome promise of Jesus

My son, when you come to serve the Lord,
prepare yourself for trials.
SIRACH 2:1

That will stop you in your tracks. It did me. Because of course, it's the exact opposite of the way we might think the spiritual life is supposed to work.

After all, when I hear the promises of the spiritual life offered in the modern world from preachers and in the spirituality section in the bookstore, it's all about making life better. Which essentially means "easier," like any other commodity that's marketed to us.

But as someone once remarked to me, "The only thing Jesus ever promised his disciples is that they would suffer."

It's not what we want to hear. But the truth is there, and something we'll admit in other parts of life: a career path, acceptance of children, committing to a relationship. What joy there is—but embarking on the journey is always going to involve more difficulties than staying in place.

And that's a promise.

Jesus, I want to follow you,
no matter what comes my way.

A time for moving on

Wherever you enter a house, stay there until you leave from there.
Whatever place does not welcome you or listen to you, leave there
and shake the dust off your feet in testimony against them.

MARK 6:10-11

I spend a lot of time on the Internet, for good or for ill, and one of the staples of Internet life is argument. One of the most energetic areas of online discussion is religion, whether it be between anti-Catholics and Catholics or between atheists and believers. Apologists from both sides debate the minutiae of Biblical authority, justification, and grace, as well as a million other topics. The discussions are heated and erudite, and I don't think I've ever heard of anyone being converted by them.

It's not that discussion and argument are useless. It's just that someone itching for a fight is usually not willing to listen, and it is better, as Jesus says, to move on—either literally, or perhaps to a different, simpler way of trying to communicate the reality of God's love.

Jesus, help me discern
where my gifts will speak
of your love most powerfully.

Opening our hearts to joy

Jesus said to her, "Mary!"
JOHN 20:16

Forget the silly novels and the wishful thinking. While the Gospels don't tell us much about Mary Magdalene, what they tell us is enough. This woman walked away from her old life to follow Jesus. Why? Because, as Luke tells us, Jesus had freed her from "seven demons"—a way of saying that her problems and her possession were total. Jesus freed her from all that, and so, in gratitude, what could she do but follow him?

And follow him she did—to the Cross, when most of the other disciples had disappeared, and then, early on that Sunday morning, to the tomb, expecting nothing but sorrow.

But her faithfulness brings her, as it does all of us, deep joy of the most surprising kind. Jesus is not dead, as she had supposed, but fully alive, calling her name.

Lord Jesus, open my heart to joy,
as I hear you call my name.

Holding each other accountable

Do you not have houses in which you can eat and drink?
Or do you show contempt for the church of God and make those
who have nothing feel ashamed? What can I say to you?
Shall I praise you? In this matter I do not praise you.

1 CORINTHIANS 11:22

A few years ago, I was working through my youthful experience in campus ministry, the good and the bad. Talking to a priest, I tried to unpack the negatives and their impact on my life. I kept interjecting, in the midst of the negatives, "But it was such a good experience of church." Finally, deep into this, the priest stopped me and said, "Maybe it wasn't such a great experience of church."

He meant that if there was a community in which individuals were doing harmful things and no one spoke up, it was a problem. It's a problem St. Paul doesn't have, by the way, as we see here: he was quite outspoken in calling Christian communities to accountability. For that's what it is: as Christians we're called to support each other, yes. But we're also called to hold ourselves and each other accountable—not to rules or regulations, but to Jesus himself, in love.

Lord, give me humility and courage
as I seek to be faithful to you.

Beware assumptions about God

*For John the Baptist came neither eating food nor drinking wine,
and you said, "He is possessed by a demon." The Son of Man came
eating and drinking and you said, "Look, he is a glutton and
a drunkard, a friend of tax collectors and sinners."*

LUKE 7:33-34

The human need to categorize and judge runs deep. Sometimes
it comes in handy, but when it comes to God, it makes nothing
but trouble.

A great deal of Jesus' preaching, and particularly his storytelling, seems directed at this very tendency. What do you assume
about God? That his forgiveness is limited? That he shares your
disdain for the outcast? That there's a statute of limitations on
redemption? That he is too vast to care about your problems?

No, Jesus says. Listen to me, and stop presuming.

His listeners here were doing the same thing: throwing out
all kinds of judgments about what a prophet should look like,
judgments that even contradicted each other and ended up
functioning as nothing but blinders to the reality of who was in
their midst, walking among them and sharing their lives.

Jesus, help me set aside
my presumptions and be open
to you as you are to me.

Give credit where credit is due

*Accompanying him were the Twelve and some women
who had been cured of evil spirits and infirmities...*

LUKE 8:1-2

In the modern way of seeing, religion is simply one part of life among many. It is the part in which we find meaning and inner peace and perhaps some moral guidance. We find time for it, we schedule it, we give it priority.

Contemplating Luke's simple, straightforward description of Jesus' female disciples, I can't help but be startled by the contrast between their stance and mine. There is no fitting faith into a busy life here; there is simply a life turned over to Jesus completely, and in gratitude. A startling move for the time, since women did not ordinarily leave their homes to follow itinerant rabbis. Radical, bold, and total, not grudging or duty-bound.

What's the difference? I think it lies in our sense of who we think deserves the credit. Mary Magdalene, Joanna, and Susanna were transformed by Jesus, and they knew it. Who do I think deserves the credit for my life and its blessings?

Lord Jesus, in gratitude, I give you more
of my heart. Give me the courage
to hand it all over to you.

Whom do you love and who loves you?

Be doers of the word and not hearers only, deluding yourselves.

JAMES 1:22

I spend a lot of time talking about faith. More to the point, I spend a lot of time talking to others about talking about faith. Lots and lots of words are exchanged, often about how to answer hard questions you're asked about what you believe.

Recently I experienced a little flash of insight—a corrective in the midst of all the words. Certainly, we want to welcome inquiries about our faith and to have the right words to answer them.

But could we think bigger, perhaps, and hope for another kind of question? For the truth is, when someone is really holy, we don't pester them with questions of why they believe and how they can justify it.

No. We stand—a little bit in awe—and we ask, not about ideas or proof, but about something else.

"Who is it," we ask. "Whom do you love and who loves you that brings you such joy?"

What a great question. Will anyone ever ask me that, I wonder?

Lord, be with me on my journey.
Let your light shine through my life.

Death's test is how not when

For whoever wishes to save his life will lose it, but whoever loses his life for my sake and that of the gospel will save it.

MARK 8:35

As the years have raced by and I've gotten older, my views on various aspects of life—and death—have slowly shifted.

As a young adult I was no different than most of my peers in my fear and denial of death's reality. A Christian in theory, I nonetheless thought of death as the worst thing that could or (of course) would happen to me. Martyrdom was admirable, but I was fairly sure that given the choice, I would choose physical life over martyrdom because, you know, at least I'd be living.

But somehow over the past years, I've started to see things in a new light.

I finally figured out that no matter what, death will come. Though it holds a great mystery, death is not the worst thing. Since death is inevitable, what matters in not when, but how. The direction I'm looking when the moment comes, whenever it comes: that's what matters.

Lord Jesus, give me the grace
to live and die for you.

Risk-taking faith

...and immediately they left their boat
and their father and followed him.

MATTHEW 4:22

Well, that sounds like everything to me. The fishing brothers left their livelihood and the rest of their family, all in response to so simple an invitation.

When I think about stories like this one, I'm seized with curiosity and even a sort of envy. I can't imagine, even for a moment, leaving everything behind based on the vague, mysterious words of someone I just met. What was it about a personal encounter with Jesus that gave birth to such trust, such risk-taking, such courage? I want to go back in time and see for myself. That, I think, would be great.

Well, too bad, because that probably won't happen. I'm here, now.

Yes, to be on the lakeshore, turn around, and see for myself would certainly be something. But do I really think that this gospel story is all about one moment lost in time?

Is this thing I'm doing a history lesson, storytelling, wishful thinking, or...could it be faith?

Lord Jesus, I know you are here.
I want to follow.

Asking questions can be faithful

Why are you so displeased with me that
you burden me with all this people?

NUMBERS 11:11

If any of us are ever tempted to believe that fidelity and holiness mean unquestioning compliance with whatever life hands us, reading this passage from Numbers will shatter that illusion, and quickly.

In the desert with grumbling Israelites, Moses lets loose in God's presence, questioning the purpose of this journey with these ever-complaining people and ending his lament with a request that God just kill him rather than make him endure any longer.

Startling, certainly, but also an intriguing invitation to enter into God's word more deeply, and to find as we do, more people just like Moses: not idealized stick figures, but real people who are frustrated, confused, fed up, and don't hesitate to confront God with those feelings and to ask why life is the way it is.

After all, we wouldn't ask a question if we didn't believe there was someone on the other end to answer it. In that struggle, too, is faith.

Lord, I give you
my questions and my frustrations,
trusting in your response.

Healing memories

They forgot the God who saved them,
who did great deeds in Egypt.

PSALM 106:21

Here's what I remember: I was a senior in high school on a weekend retreat in a retreat house in Atlanta. It was silent, at least in theory, and one of the things we'd heard a talk on was using Scripture in prayer. Specifically, we'd been given the assignment of going back to our rooms, or wherever we liked on the grounds, and using the technique we'd been taught to read and pray John's account of the Passion.

So I did. I remember sitting on the floor of my room, entering into that moment. I also remember going into the eucharistic chapel later, a chapel strewn with large pillows and at that point empty but for me and the Lord.

That's what I remember and have never forgotten. At times when I have all sorts of questions about God, and I'm tempted to turn away, I remember.

Loving God, may I never
forget your presence.

How far from Christ will I go?

What profit would there be for one
to gain the whole world and forfeit his life?

MATTHEW 16:26

"Reality shows" have been all the rage on television. They aren't documentaries, but mostly contests of some sort in which participants usually engage in all sorts of humiliating acts to win cash: choose a spouse, be chosen as one, find one's biological father, trade spouses, compete to be the prime heir to your elderly relation's will, or simply consume some slugs.

The mind boggles and can't help but wonder: how far will people go? What are they willing to lose in order to get their face on television and grab some more cash?

Like so much else, it's an intriguing call to look in the mirror as well. How far will I go to obtain whatever worldly things I value? How many steps away from Christ will I dare to take, telling myself that I haven't gone too far yet?

Lord Jesus, help me to see my life
as you do, for what it is,
and what it can be.

To know and to live the truth

And demons also came out from many,
shouting, "You are the Son of God."
LUKE 4:41

I was raised in a household that valued knowledge very high-ly, so it makes sense that the first glimmers of interest in faith in my life were intellectual. From early on, I wanted to know. My fifth-grade CCD teacher, fed up with the curriculum he was given, pulled out a Baltimore Catechism. I was delighted. I wanted to know. My ninth-grade religion teacher was strict and hard-core, having us read Vatican II documents and pour over the Scriptures. I loved it. I wanted to know.

And still, I want to know. I find a book on a library or store shelf and think that at last I've found the key—this author has got it, and if I simply immerse myself in his or her words and understand them, I'll know, and I'll be happy.

But, as this Gospel story shows us, even the demons know. Even the demons understand who Jesus is. You could say, intel-lectually, they "get" him.

A disciple? That's different. Disciples know, yes. But disciples do something else: they live.

Jesus, I put my life
in your hands, and I follow.

May God's vision of me be my vision

Remember no more the sins of my youth;
remember me only in light of your love.

PSALM 25:7

A couple of my children are getting pretty old, which means that some of their childhood memories are more vivid than others. Twenty years is a long time ago. There are times in which one of my young adult sons will say to me, "Remember when I..." and they'll rattle off some offense they committed way back when.

Nope. More often than not, I don't remember. And even if I did, it wouldn't matter much. The past is over and done with. It might impact the present, but I can't let it define it—for my sons or for myself, either.

I can't let myself be burdened by guilt over sins that I committed yesterday, sins that God has forgiven and for which I've been reconciled.

I'm not going to define my children by things they did a decade ago. God doesn't define me that way, either.

Isn't it time to let God's vision of me be my vision as well?

Forgiving God, release me from
the chains of guilt and let me live
in the present light of your love.

Love calls for help from God

*In this is love: not that we have loved God, but that
he loved us and sent his Son as expiation for our sins.
Beloved, if God so loved us, we also must love one another.*

1 JOHN 4:10-11

Self-reliant, independent, and autonomous: it's what we're all
supposed to be. You can do great things, we're told, if you but dig
deep and rely on your own inner resources. Everything you need
to succeed and live well is within you.

Well, maybe not.

Perhaps you've found, as I have, that one's own inner resources can only go so far. Mine are limited by my own point of view,
my needs and desires, and, yes, my selfishness.

That's why I need God to expand my vision and deepen my
strength. It's why, when faced with the challenges of real love,
rather than trying to do it all on my own, I turn to God and let
him love through me, as only he can do—without limit.

God of love, live in me.

Idolatry

Their idols are silver and gold,
the work of human hands.
Their makers shall be like them,
all who trust in them.

PSALM 115:4, 8

Ah yes… idols. What are yours made of?

Mine are constructed out of various materials: Some are paper—books that I want to see published, not just because I hope they will help others but because, secretly, I believe their existence will validate mine. Some are made of flesh and blood: human beings whose approval would somehow give my life more purpose. Others are nothing but numbers: what I think I must weigh in order to be happy with myself, sales figures, numbers of readers, the cushion in the bank account.

What is it exactly, do I think they will do for me? Have they proven themselves trustworthy in the past? Have they forgiven my sins, brought me lasting peace, and will they give me eternal life?

So why, I wonder, do I insist on worshipping them?

Lord of all, turn my heart toward you.
Help me trust in you and you alone
to save me and bring me peace.

On time

*Immorality or any impurity or greed must not even
be mentioned among you, as is fitting among holy ones...*
EPHESIANS 5:3

I think a lot about time: how much time I have today, how much
time is left to me on the planet, how quickly time has passed and
where the time has gone.

Answers: not enough; a lot, I hope; way too fast; and I wish
I knew.

So time holds a lot of mystery for me, but one thing that's not
mysterious is how much I have the ability to waste. No, it's not
that busyness is required every minute—after all, God rested on
the seventh day, and so should I.

It's the question of where my head was and what my priori-
ties were. I look at Paul's words in that spirit. Why fill my head
and waste my time with matters that bring me down, when I
could be filling that same space in a way that brings me closer
to God?

Lord, clear my mind, so that
I might give it over to you.

Beyond words

One day to the next conveys that message;
one night to the next imparts that knowledge.
There is no word or sound; no voice is heard.

PSALM 19:3-4

If you've ever really loved, you know how frustrating words of love can be. After all, those words are so worn out, so overused, not to speak of misused, that real love demands something else, something beyond words.

I suppose it's just true that the more important and more profound the thought, the less adequate words are to the task. Only a life, only presence, mysterious yet true, will—can—do it justice.

That's why these words of the psalmist stop me in my tracks. He knows this, he sees it. God is too much for words, and more importantly, if we really pay attention to what's going on around us, words are barely necessary to know God's love and presence. God's nurture and care are beyond the power of words to express.

Lord, in silence, I am present to you
in whatever way you speak to me today.

Matters of life and death

For to me life is Christ, and death is gain. If I go on living in the flesh, that means fruitful labor for me. And I do not know which I shall choose.

PHILIPPIANS 1:21-22

I've not yet directly confronted death myself, but like anyone with more than forty years behind her, I've had minor wake-up calls from my own body. I've had to consider the rare, but still possible, consequences of childbirth. And I've passed the scene of an accident minutes after it occurred often enough to have my share of "There but for the grace of God go I" moments.

When I do think about death, I'm torn like Paul. For while my faith rejoices in eternal life with Christ, no way do I want to leave my kids, especially now. The thought horrifies me, not for my sake, but for theirs. There is much more "fruitful labor" to be done.

It's good, because it focuses me on why I'm here in the first place.

Jesus, be glorified through me today.

The word abides year after year

*And the Word became flesh and made his dwelling
among us, and we saw his glory, the glory as of the
Father's only Son, full of grace and truth.*

JOHN 1:14

When I was ten years old, I went outside on the first day of the new year with a small bottle. I held it up in the air, put the cap on, taped a label on the outside, and wrote "1970" on it. It fascinated me to think that perhaps I could capture a slice of time and keep it forever.

We can't, of course. Another year has passed, and with it countless moments of joy, sorrow, and routine. Those moments fly away; they can't be captured in a bottle, no matter how hard we try. But I think what does remain, what does mysteriously stay with us and grow, is the glory of the Word we've seen this past year. People and moments have come and gone, but the Word has made his dwelling, and he remains with me.

I can take nothing else into the new year, really, except Christ. And that's enough.

Jesus, thank you for the
past year. I pray that I may grow
ever closer to you in the next.

Moving past the grief of death

And they were overwhelmed with grief.
MATTHEW 17:23

I admit that far too often, I can identify with Jesus' apostles here. They have just heard Jesus predict his Passion. He will be killed, he says, and then raised on the third day.

But wait—he says he will be raised. Why do they still grieve?

For the same reason, I suppose, so many of us still fear death. For me, it happens if I linger over the obituary page too long or find myself stopped at the intersection where there's a huge cemetery taking up blocks and blocks on my right. I've heard the good news. I think I believe it. But I still grieve.

The apostles "grieved" because they did not understand. They couldn't—it was too startling to envision. They hadn't encountered the Risen Jesus yet.

And so it is with me. When I'm gripped with a fear of death, I refocus. I consider the Resurrection. Do I believe this really happened? Yes, I do. So what's the problem?

Perhaps, like the apostles, for it all to be real, I need to meet the living, risen Christ. Again.

Jesus, may I embrace the
new life you offer me.

Reviving warm memories

Yet I will remember the covenant I made with you when you were a girl, and I will set up an everlasting covenant with you.

EZEKIEL 16:60

My youngest son is three now, and sometimes when my daughter and I are with him, I ask her, "Remember when he was tiny and couldn't even hold his head up?"

And she'll say, point blank, "No."

Well, the truth is, I barely remember myself. The past blends with the present, and one baby blends in with three others, and time just keeps moving on.

Sometimes, though, we have to intentionally walk back to the memories to remind ourselves of what this love is all about. The memories of the sleeping baby, the happy first years of marriage and family life, the carefree days of firm friendship help us refocus on what can still be, even if our hearts have grown faint.

For us, too, it might be a comfort to know that when we feel we've strayed, God's covenant love for us is ever new. God gazes at us as we in our memories looked upon that sleeping baby, our hearts bursting with love.

Lord, open my heart to
your loving embrace.

The prayer of the whole wide world

For where two or three are gathered together
in my name, there am I in the midst of them.

MATTHEW 18:20

I've recently started thinking about prayer in a new way. For most of my life, despite some good intentions, I've thought of prayer as being about not much more than me and God. My needs, my questions, God's answers. To me.

But over the last year, I began looking not only into what Scripture says about prayer, but into the Liturgy of the Hours, that cycle of prayers that mainly priests and religious have prayed for centuries.

In the process, something struck me, and pretty hard: I am not alone. I am a tiny part of something that's really huge: it's called creation, and as St. Paul says, it's a creation that is being reconciled in Christ. The prayer of the Church—all the individual prayers, all the Masses, all the chanting of the Liturgy of the Hours, all over the world—is a part of that reconciling, as we praise God, thank him, and hold each other up before him.

And in the midst of us—two, three, and millions beyond that—is Christ.

Lord, I join my prayer to those
of millions more today, in your praise.

The shelf life of today's urgencies

*But what profit did you get then from the
things of which you are now ashamed?*

ROMANS 6:21

As part of a parish discussion group's program, we were asked to share something about our lives that we might do differently if we had the chance. I have no idea what I said, but the comment of another woman, well into her 70s, stuck with me ever since: she said, "I wouldn't worry so much about how my house looked. I'd spend more time just being with my children as they were growing up. I can't believe I thought housekeeping was more important than just stopping and listening to and playing with my children." Which explains the condition of my own house, twenty years later, if you ever stop by and look.

It's a good criterion to use when we make choices. How am I going to feel about this tomorrow? In ten years? As my life comes to a close? What will this have brought me: life—or a kind of small, sad death?

Lord, help me shape my life
in way that reflects your love.

"Help me live in joyful expectation"

*Gird your loins and light your lamps and be like servants
who await their master's return from a wedding,
ready to open immediately when he comes and knocks.*

LUKE 12:35-36

The spot of land that I call home must have the most unpredictable weather in the country. More times than I can count, the television weather reporters have filled the air with dire warnings about huge snowstorms brewing, ready to blanket and immobilize us for days. Of course, everyone rushes to the grocery store. Within hours, the shelves are cleared of water, milk, and bread. Followed by, also more times than I can count, days of sunny skies. (And perhaps many, many dishes of bread pudding.)

It works the other way, too. One Christmas Eve, we went to bed told to expect nothing except a chill the next day. We awoke to a foot of snow. We didn't expect it, and most of us weren't prepared.

We can be certain that what Jesus warns us about—the moment we will be called to account for ourselves before God—will, indeed, come to pass. If not tonight, it will be sooner than we think. Are we ready?

Lord, help me live a life
of joyful expectation, awaiting
fullness of life with you.

So many to thank for my faith!

We give thanks to God always for all of you, remembering you in our prayers, unceasingly calling to mind your work of faith…

1 THESSALONIANS 1:2-3

For whose witness and faith should I thank God? My parents who brought me to the waters of baptism, who saw to my religious education, however sporadic it may have been. The Southern Baptist friend in the eighth grade who asked me a million "whys" about being Catholic and wouldn't take "I don't know" for an answer. My friends in the college campus ministry. My friend who's fought three kinds of cancer, and emerged faith intact. My husband. My children, who revealed to me the breadth and depth of human love, leaving me humbled before what must be the reality of God's love.

Then, of course, the list must include those who formed all of these people, and then their own teachers and witnesses. And so the list extends across space and time, so that in the end, I can in all honesty, truth and joy, join my own prayer across twenty centuries and echo the words of Paul.

Lord, today I thank you for those who sacrificed so that I might know you.

Unlikely Christian heroes

Let no one have contempt for your youth, but set an example for those who believe, in speech, conduct, love, faith, and purity.

1 TIMOTHY 4:12

Who can teach us about faith? Who are the witnesses whose words speak most powerfully? Isn't it odd that so much of the time, it's the most unlikely characters?

It's Paul, the man who used to persecute Christians and indeed witnessed the stoning of the first Christian martyr. It's the young Timothy whom that same Paul encourages here. It's Francis of Assisi, the radical son of a most solid citizen. It's Dorothy Day, twice pregnant outside of marriage, once aborted. It's Mother Teresa, spending her time on the most hopeless and helpless cases.

Our culture tempts us constantly to seek wisdom only from its self-defined best and brightest, successful and mainstream. That doesn't seem to be the Christian way—which, when you think about it, makes sense for a people who see God's love revealed in his broken body on a cross.

Loving God, open my heart to the ways you move in the world, no matter how unlikely they may seem to me at first.

How can I become fruitful again?

But as for the seed that fell on rich soil, they are the ones who, when they have heard the word, embrace it with a generous and good heart, and bear fruit through perseverance.

LUKE 8:15

Listening to Jesus tell the Parable of the Sower, we quite naturally fit ourselves and those we know into the categories Jesus describes. Most of us probably would say that our lives at one time or another have been composed of every kind of soil Jesus describes. We've been hard and infertile, we've been rocky and shallow, we've allowed weedy distractions to choke out our faith. There have even been times when we've been fertile.

Rather than focusing on those times of drought and withering, we may find it more helpful to consider those moments in life when we've really allowed God's grace to take root in our lives. What was happening then? What frame of mind made our spirits so fertile and open to God's seed? What do we need to let go of in order to be fruitful once again?

Lord, give me the grace to
be unafraid of the bountiful fruit
you want to grow in my life.

Controlling my happiness

I fostered them like one
who raises an infant to his cheeks…
HOSEA 11:4

Control. If I just had a little more of it, I'd be happier. Sound familiar? How often we blame our misery on a lack of control over our lives: we need to get a handle on our schedules; we need to get more control over our family lives and those darn kids; we really should get healthier so we can have more control over our bodies and, ultimately, how and when we're going to die. If only we could control that….

But if I had control over all of it, if my house were immaculate, if my deadlines approached in a leisurely manner, if I had perfect kids, if I were never surprised by anything, and always prepared—if all that happened, God wouldn't love me any more. Or any less.

Clean house or messy house, a day that's planned or just experienced, I remain God's child, God's beloved infant, raised to his cheeks and bathed by the warmth of his heart's love and mercy.

Control has its place, to be sure. But not if it makes me forget who I really am.

Lord, embrace me today
and always. I need it.

God's messy, beautiful house

So then you are no longer strangers and sojourners,
but you are fellow citizens with the holy ones
and members of the household of God...
EPHESIANS 2:19

We travel quite a bit and so have the opportunity to attend churches all around the country. Often, at the beginning of Mass, the celebrant invites visitors to make themselves known by raising their hands or even announcing where they're from. A very well-intentioned practice, to be sure, but one that always makes us think a little.

When we attend another Catholic church, are we really "visitors"? After all, we're not baptized into a particular parish. We're baptized into Christ through his Church. So aren't I actually a parishioner at every parish in the world, from St. Peter's to Mumbai to Sao Paulo?

I think I am, and so are you, and that's a pretty amazing and humbling thought to me: that when we're at Mass together, even if I came from around the corner and you got here on an airplane, there are no visitors or strangers. There's only a chance to welcome another brother or sister into another room in this huge, messy but beautiful household of God.

Lord, open my heart to
all my sisters and brothers.

111

Am I doing enough?

*[Jesus] said to them, "There is no need for them to go away;
give them some food yourselves." But they said to him,
"Five loaves and two fish are all we have here."
Then he said, "Bring them here to me…"*

MATTHEW 14:16-18

When confronted with the Gospel, I often wonder if I am doing
enough. It's not a matter of scrupulosity or of believing that my
salvation depends on my own efforts. Rather, I listen to the call
of Jesus and I look, quite honestly, at the comfort in which I live,
and it seems to me that being a disciple requires more than I am
giving.

Surely, I think, I must go off and do something else—something grand. But then who would read the bedtime stories?

Yes, the call of Jesus is to also dig deeper and open ourselves
to greater, more sacrificial love. And sometimes we're called to
leave where we are to do that.

But other times, there is no need for us to go away, no need
to do anything but look where I am now, hand what I find over
to Jesus, and let him work with what I have, where I am right
now.

Jesus, take what I have and
bless it so others will be fed.

He is with us always

But now, compelled by the Spirit, I am going to Jerusalem. What will happen to me there I do not know...

ACTS 20:22

It seems I have spent much of my life surrounded by young people looking anxiously toward the future: students, my children, their friends. Currently, it is my daughter, who is researching colleges intently, determined to find the "perfect" place and convinced that if she makes the wrong choice, her life will be thrown off course. Maybe forever!

What she doesn't understand, but will eventually, is that while it's true that some situations are better than others for us, God is with us in all of them. We do our part to discern and decide— "compelled by the Spirit," as Paul was—but the truth is, just like Paul, we just don't know what will happen to us when we arrive. And also like Paul, in all of those places, we find peace, not in where we are, but in who's with us—always.

Lord, I don't know what the
future holds, but I'm joyful that
you'll be with me there.

Asking the right question

He said to him the third time, "Simon, son of John,
do you love me?" Peter was distressed that he had said
to him a third time, "Do you love me?" and he said to him,
"Lord, you know everything; you know that I love you."
[Jesus] said to him, "Feed my sheep."
JOHN 21:17

You can take all kinds of tests and inventories that will help you decide how to spend your time, resources, and money. Personality types, charisms, gifts, talents. You can figure it all out with the right assessment, if you want.

All of that might be helpful at one time or another. But if we're not careful, we might be looking for the answer to the wrong question. If you're like me, that question is usually a variation of, "What's going to make me happy?" Perhaps that's the wrong question. Perhaps the question we should be answering isn't even our question at all.

"Do you love me?"

Lord, I love you.
What do you want me to do?

Looking into the mirror

Be doers of the word and not hearers only, deluding yourselves.

JAMES 1:22

Helping a teenager stay on task is no easy matter, especially when she's working on a computer hooked to the Internet. I always tell her I can tell if she's working or not by how fast she's typing. If the fingers are racing, that means she's chatting, not working. And it's true.

So I get frustrated with her and talk about her own goals and what she is capable of accomplishing and how she really needs to be more disciplined. I wonder when she will get the picture. And then I look down at my own computer, four or five browser windows open to various blogs and news sites and online magazines. While my word processing screen with work half-done sits quietly, having been waiting unattended for some time now.

How can I expect her to do what I've not mastered? How many other things can I speak easily about—like the importance of prayer, charity, and love—deluding myself that I don't need a talking-to as well?

Lord, help me confront
my own weaknesses.

Living in hope

We do not want you to be unaware, brothers, about those who have fallen asleep, so that you may not grieve like the rest, who have no hope.

1 THESSALONIANS 4:13

We moved to a new city about a year ago, but some time before the actual move, I spent a couple of weeks in another part of the same town. During that first sojourn, there was a certain busy area that seemed to be a great distance away. When we would drive down there to shop, it was like a foreign place and I couldn't imagine being a regular there at all. As it turned out, we ended up living there. It's the same place, but I'm reoriented, and now it is home.

All of us—believers or not—dwell in the same reality of life and death. But in this same landscape, we who have hope, as Paul says, think differently about the apparent sadness of death. It is the same place, but knowing that this place and all within belong to God, we are reoriented and live, not in cold grief and fear, but at home in hope.

Loving God, help me trust
in your eternal love.

"Follow me"

As Jesus passed on from there, he saw a man named Matthew
sitting at the customs post. He said to him, "Follow me."

MATTHEW 9:9

In Rome, you can see the famed Caravaggio painting of this
moment in the back corner of a smaller church in the center
city. Out of the deep shadows steps Jesus. His outstretched hand
points in the direction of a group of men at a table, and one
of those men extends his own hand, gesturing back towards
himself.

Me?

In Rome you also see this: churches built over the tombs of
young, innocent martyrs, magnificent churches built by church-
men and noblemen anxious to compensate for their sins, set
snugly along cobblestone streets trod by pilgrims rich and poor,
saints and sinners, and all in between. All of us, some for better
reasons than others, responding out of our own weakness to the
call.

Me?

Jesus, yes. I will follow you.

Slow down, smell the flowers

You have sown much, but have brought in little;
you have eaten, but have not been satisfied;
You have drunk, but have not been exhilarated;
have clothed yourselves, but not been warmed...

HAGGAI 1:6

My seven-year-old and I went to see a huge model train exhibit. He walked around the large track fairly quickly, and announced there was nothing much to see and he was ready to go.

I made him go back, but this time I pointed out the activities of the tiny detailed figures, buildings, and scenes. Once he realized that there was more going on than he had first realized, he took off, eager to study what he had missed the first time.

My life can be very busy, but at times the busyness involves so much skimming of the surface that I end my day having done all I should do, but still unsatisfied, cold, and anything but exhilarated. God is in the details, they say. Perhaps I need to slow down and consider those details.

God, help me live in an awareness
of your constant presence.

Into the light of understanding

*While they were all amazed at his every deed, he said
to his disciples, "Pay attention to what I am telling you.
The Son of Man is to be handed over to men."
But they did not understand this saying.*

LUKE 9:43-45

My oldest son sent me a text message on my cell phone before
Mass. "I totaled my car... " it began, but I read no further. I
closed my phone, mildly annoyed, believing what I had read was
a jokey excuse for being late. He showed up a bit later, frazzled,
but unhurt—in a police car.

Suffering, pain, and darkness. No one wants to hear about it,
and even when we are forced to confront it, we still find it difficult to comprehend. In a dark, ironic culture, we can even treat
it as a joke.

Reality remains, though, even if we try to turn the phone off
or claim we don't get it. Only if we pay attention to him will we
be able to walk the whole journey, into light, understanding at
last.

Jesus, I will walk with you
on this difficult road.

God's unchanging love

It is God who governs the world with justice,
who judges the peoples with fairness.

PSALM 9:9

If there is anything about parenting that, after twenty-six years of it, is starting to wear me out, it is adjudicating disputes. (That and trying to get children to eat food that isn't breaded or is a color other than brown or white.)

I'm just really, really tired of tussles over toys and territory and what he said or she said. I hate to admit it, but, too much of the time, I'm pretty indifferent to who really deserves what and will take some peace and quiet at almost any price. Awful, isn't it?

Thank God—and really, thank God—that God is unchanging in love, mercy, and justice and will never become indifferent to the realities of my life. I can count on God to attend to the truth of my life and never brush me off because he's got something better to do. Perhaps in my gratitude, I could learn something.

Dear God, hear the
pleading of my heart.

In the midst of sadness...

Jesus asked him, "What do you want me to do for you?"
He replied, "Lord, please let me see."

LUKE 18:40-41

Several months ago my husband died suddenly at age fifty while running on the treadmill at the gym. I think of him all the time, of course, but on this date especially, because it is his birthday. My prayer in the immediate wake of his death was, not surprisingly, full of questions, confusion, sadness, and even anger.

At one point I was praying the Liturgy of the Hours centered on the psalms that express hunger and yearning for God, for God's peace, for life with God. These were the prayers my husband had offered so faithfully for years, since he was a daily Mass-goer and indeed prayed the Liturgy of the Hours for three decades. He had prayed—daily—for the fullness of God's peace and love, and, like the blind man, for healing and wholeness. In a flash, a truth came to me: his prayers have been answered. A reason, even in the midst of sadness, to be grateful for birth— and rebirth.

Jesus, please let me see.

Praise God as sacrifice

Offer to God praise as your sacrifice...
PSALM 50:14

On first glance, this might seem too easy. Even a bit of a cop-out. How could praise be the equivalent of a concrete sacrifice? Compared to the first of your flock or harvest, your money, or your time, it doesn't seem as if saying words of praise to God could require anything of me.

Ah, but maybe it does. When things are not going well. When life hasn't turned out as I planned or hoped. When I'm experiencing loss or disappointment. Then yes, perhaps putting aside my own desires, plans, and conception of what life should be like does, indeed, require a sacrifice. A far greater sacrifice than anything concrete or material, in fact. As St. Ignatius wrote in his prayer, "Take, Lord, receive all my liberty." It might be the greatest sacrifice I can make today.

Lord, I praise you for everything in my life, past and present.